Contents:

Photography:

GLEN S. AXELROD: 2-3, 6, 10-11, 18-19, 27, 29, 30-31, 34-35, 38-39, 42, 44-45, 46-47, 48, 50-51, 78-79, 83, 86-87, 90-91, 94-95. MARY BLOOM: 15, 58-59. J.C. PAPAS: 26 (bottom). MERVIN F. ROBERTS: 18 (top), 70 (top). LINDA SMOTHERS: 26 (top). RUDY VACA: 17, 52-53. WENDY WINSTED: 14-15, 23, 60-61, 66-67, 70-71, 75, 82,, 84-85.

ISBN 0-87666-930-5

5-26-05

© Copyright 1981 by T.F.H. Publications, Inc. Ltd.

Distributed in the UNITED STATES by T.F.H. Publications, Inc., 211 West Sylvania Avenue, Neptune City, NJ 07753; in CANADA by H & L Pet Supplies Inc., 27 Kingston Crescent, Kitchener, Ontario N2B 2T6; Rolf C. Hagen Ltd., 3225 Sartelon Street, Montreal 382 Quebec; in ENGLAND by T.F.H. (Great Britain) Ltd., 11 Ormside Way, Holmethorpe Industrial Estate, Redhill, Surrey RH1 2PX; in AUSTRALIA AND THE SOUTH PACIFIC by T.F.H. (Australia) Pty. Ltd., Box 149, Brookvale 2100 N.S.W., Australia; in NEW ZEALAND by Ross Haines & Son, Ltd., 18 Monmouth Street, Grey Lynn, Auckland 2 New Zealand; in SINGAPORE AND MALAYSIA by MPH Distributors Pte., 71-77 Stamford Road, Singapore 0617; in the PHILIPPINES by Bio-Research, 5 Lippay Street, San Lorenzo Village, Makati, Rizal; in SOUTH AFRICA by Multipet Pty. Ltd., 30 Turners Avenue, Durban 4001. Published by T.F.H. Publications Inc., Ltd., the British Crown Colony of Hong Kong. THIS IS THE 1983 EDITION.

FERRETS

WENDY WINSTED

In general, ferrets get along well with people and of course (left and below) with each other.

Introduction

It is not the purpose of this book to go into detail about the origin, evolution or history of the fitch ferret. This information is available from numerous other sources. Instead, I intend to provide a *practical* guide to keeping a ferret as a house pet and to share with you some of the knowledge I have gained from my experiences and collected from numerous other ferret owners over the past eight years. I hope that it will help you to enjoy your pet as much as I have enjoyed mine.

I would like to give a few special words of thanks to Gilman and Gary Marshall, who have been breeding ferrets for the past 42 years, and to Dr. Emil Dolensek, Chief Veterinarian for the New York Zoological Society (the Bronx Zoo), for all the help and advice they have given me through the years. Without their help this book would not have been possible.

I would also like to thank Dr. Constance Martin, Professor of Endocrinology at Hunter College of the City University of New York, for her help with the section about reproduction and Kinnereth Ellentuck, my downstairs neighbor and a ferret owner, for her help with the ferret play and personality section.

A BRIEF BACKGROUND

The subway doors open and I quickly step inside and take a seat. A middle-aged man wearing a business suit stares at me for a few minutes and says something to the woman accompanying him. Then they both get up and come and take a seat next to me.

"Excuse me, miss," says the man. "Are those things in your purse baby raccoons?"

"No, they're full-grown ferrets."

"Parrots?"

"No, parrots are birds. These are *ferrets.*"

"What's a ferret?"

"It's a domestic animal in the mink and otter family," I tell him.

"They're really cute, but don't you think they'd be happier out in the woods?" he asks somewhat belligerently. "I mean, I don't think it's right to take animals out of their natural habitat and make them live in the city. It's cruel; they should be free."

"They're *in* their natural habitat," I explain. "Ferrets are *domestic* animals. A wolf is wild–a Yorkshire Terrier is domesticated. Ferrets wouldn't like to be left out in the woods any more than a Yorkshire Terrier would. In fact, the dark one doesn't even *like* to go outdoors. They were born inside. They don't know anything about the woods."

"How do you *know* it doesn't like to be outdoors?" the man asks, still not quite ready to give up.

"Because when I take her out in my brother's backyard and put her down she runs right back to the door and stands there looking up at the doorknob–waiting to be let back in."

"She doesn't mind being on the subway? You'd think she'd be afraid of all this noise."

"No, ferrets aren't nervous animals. Besides, she's used to it.

She doesn't really mind being anywhere indoors, and she doesn't mind being outdoors as long as she can stay in my bag. She likes to look around. The other one likes to go outdoors as long as she can go back in the bag when she gets tired."

"Well, they're certainly beautiful animals," he continues in a more amiable tone.

"They're just absolutely darling," the lady with him chimes in. "What are their names?"

"The one with white feet is Melinda and the darker one is McGuinn."

"Are they good pets?"

"Excellent pets," I assure her.

"Do you have to keep them in a cage?"

"No, they just run loose around the house, although sometimes I put them in a cage when I clean because otherwise they chase the vacuum cleaner and get underfoot."

"Do they tear things up?"

"No, they don't really chew on anything except soft rubber and kitchen sponges, and they don't sharpen their claws like cats, so they aren't destructive animals," I tell her, leaving out the part about the big hole Melinda dug in my avocado plant just a few days ago. (Like many other ferrets, Melinda especially enjoys hole digging. McGuinn, though, shows no interest whatsoever in such activities.)

"Do they bite?" she asks as she pokes her finger in McGuinn's face.

"No," I answer, but my reply isn't necessary, because both ferrets are just sniffing her fingers as they generally do when people poke at them.

"Aren't you afraid they'll run away?"

"No, they're used to being on the subway, and they know they aren't allowed to get down."

"May I hold one?" she asks.

I hand her Melinda, who, while not impressed with the lady, takes an immediate interest in her handbag and struggles to free herself from the lady's grasp.

"Oh no," the lady cries in alarm. "She's trying to get away!"

"Actually she just wants to look in your purse," I explain.

1. The author being kissed by her ferret McGuinn; once a pet ferret gets to know and trust you, it can demonstrate affection. 2. Four of the author's ferrets traveling in their "mobile home."

2 →

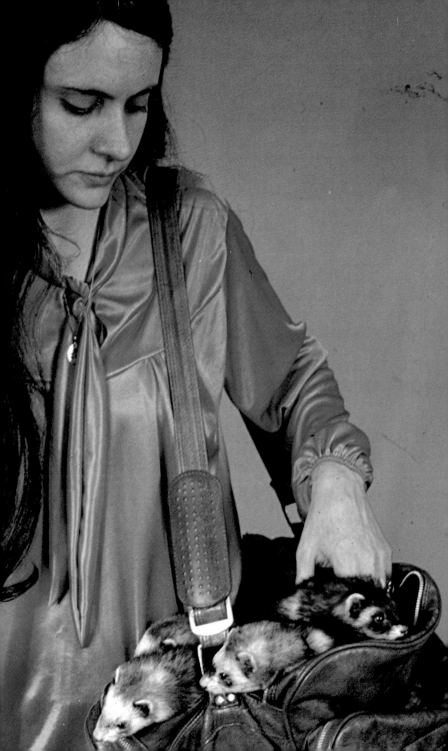

"Ferrets are always nosey that way."

"Is it all right to let her look?"

"Sure. I don't mind if you don't."

The woman turns loose of Melinda, who then immediately sticks her head inside the purse.

"What do they eat?" the man asks.

"Cat food mostly, but they like people food as well."

I look back at the handbag to see that Melinda has disappeared.

"Whoops, sorry about that!" I apologize as a hairbrush comes flying out of the purse. "Sometimes she likes to rearrange things too."

"Melinda, come out of there," I call to her. She pokes her head out and looks at me. "Come here Melinda—that's enough looking," I tell her.

She crawls out of the handbag and comes over to my lap, where she curls up for a nap.

"Did you see that?" the man exclaims. "She's trained. She minds!"

The woman is also duly impressed, so I don't tell them that *I'm* almost as surprised as *they* are. All of my ferrets have learned to come when called—except in a situation such as this when they are investigating something new, and then they become temporarily deaf!

"Oh, look, she's going to sleep," coos the lady. "Isn't that just the sweetest thing you've ever seen in your life! Wait'll I tell the girls in the office about this. They won't believe it!"

"Well, this is our stop," says the man as they get up to go. "Good luck with your little pets," he smiles at me as he steps out of the car.

"Yes, good luck with them," the lady calls out over her shoulder.

"Thanks. Have a nice day," I say as the door closes behind them.

An elderly man seated across from me smiles.

"Haven't seen one of those since I was in the Old Country fifty years ago," he tells me with a thick accent. "We used to use them for hunting. Never seen a gentle one like that though; the ones we had were big and mean. Couldn't pick one up without gloves on or he'd bite you right through to the bone."

"Do you mind if I pet one?" he asks me, getting up.

"No, go ahead."

He scratches McGuinn on the head. She looks up at him and yawns.

"Well, I'll be. Now I've seen everything," he chuckles to himself.

The train stops, the doors open, and several people step into the car.

"Are those monkeys that girl has?" I hear one of them ask his companion.

"No, they're squirrels," his companion answers knowledgeably.

"They look like 'possums to me," I hear from somewhere off in the background.

"Are those skunks?" someone finally asks me.

"No, skunks are black with white stripes," I tell her, no longer amazed at the question, as I've learned over the years that many people have absolutely no idea of what a skunk looks like!

"They're ferrets," I continue.

"What are ferrets?" she asks inevitably, and I start all over again.

I must have gone through similar conversations at least a thousand times in the eight years that I have owned and bred fitch ferrets. Ferrets love meeting people and going new places, so I usually take one or two of mine with me wherever I go—from the neighborhood grocery store to the college classroom as well as on trips out of town. I find that they are easy to travel with because they are small and quiet and will readily adapt to almost anything. In fact, my ferrets are so quiet and well-behaved at school that my endocrinology professor, who knew that I raised ferrets, did not notice until the last day of class that I always had one or two sleeping on my lap—and I always sat in the front row!

They can also disappear, if need be, into my shoulder bag, which doubles as their mobile home—complete with bed and litter pan. When the bag is zippered shut no one ever even suspects their presence. In this way they have been smuggled onto buses and airplanes and into nightclubs and movies. I've found, however, that they are usually welcome and even popular in

1. Ferrets make wonderful pets for mature individuals and also (2) for children—but children, of course, must be old enough and responsible enough before having ferrets entrusted to their care.

2 →

most of the places I go. Their undying curiosity makes them fun to watch, and, because they are so unusual, they are an ideal conversation piece and a good way to meet people. My ferrets have introduced me to several people who subsequently became very close friends—and ferret owners as well!

I presently have six ferrets who are permanent members of the household, four females (McGuinn, Sally, Melinda, and her daughter McKendree) and two males (Melinda's sons David and Daniel, who serve as the local studs). There always seem to be baby ferret kits coming and going, as well as various abandoned adults looking for new homes, so at times the ferret population in my kitchen has risen as high as 34. Fortunately most of the 34 were babies and didn't stay long!

FERRETS IN GENERAL

Ferrets, while considered exotic pets ("exotic" here meaning oddball or strange, not necessarily foreign), are not wild animals. They are a domesticated strain of a Eurasian weasel, *Mustela putorius,* the polecat, an animal that has a number of different subspecies scattered over a wide geographic region. The exact subspecies or combination of subspecies of *M. putorius* from which the domesticated animal that we call the ferret descended is not known, and opinion on this subject varies.

Some zoologists believe, although it is not known for certain, that the Egyptians were the first to keep ferrets, which they domesticated around 1500 B.C. to catch mice. The ferret was later replaced by the cat, which became more popular for rodent extermination. The first ferrets were brought to the United States from Spain in the 1870's.

The ferret got its name from the Latin word *furritus,* meaning "little fur thief," probably because of its fame as an expert hunter. The ferret is a member of the family Mustelidae along with its cousins the otter, mink, weasel, martin, ermine, badger, and skunk. All members of this family have scent glands located on either side of the rectum. (The family name is derived from the Latin word for musk.) These glands produce a strong-smelling musk which is secreted when the animal is frightened or otherwise excited and may play a role in locating a mate during the mating season. Unlike the skunk, which produces by far the strongest and most unpleasant anal gland fluid of any animal in this family, the ferret is not capable of spraying.

While many ferrets do have dark or "black" feet, they should not be confused with the now nearly extinct native American black-footed ferret *(Mustela nigripes)*, which is a wild species and entirely different.

Fitch ferrets are not wild animals, so they do not have any of the many disadvantages that most wild pets have, such as nervousness, shyness around strangers, or the tendency to bite. In addition, ferrets, unlike most wild animals, do not become unmanageable when they reach sexual maturity. They are gentle enough for young children and are ideal pets for those who want something different and unusual.

Having been successfully domesticated for many years, pet-stock ferrets can easily be acclimated to handling by people.

The color variety of ferret you choose is of much less importance than the animal's sex and basic soundness of body and temperament.

Choosing Your Ferret

Ferrets obtained at any age can make satisfactory pets, and how attached to you they become usually has more to do with the amount of attention they receive and their own inherited personality than the age at which they were acquired.

While all ferrets like people, some are more "people-oriented" than others. I got my first ferret, McGuinn, when she was just three and a half weeks old, before she had even opened her eyes. I bottle-fed her for three weeks, thinking that if I served as her sur-

rogate mother she would become even more attached to me than usual. I had no other ferret to compare her with until I got Melinda about a year later. Melinda was ten weeks old when I bought her. For the first few days she was afraid of me and would run and hide under the refrigerator when I tried to pick her up. After that initial adjustment period she became more affectionate than McGuinn had ever been. When she got tired of playing she would come and curl up on my lap to sleep, while McGuinn had always preferred to nap under the sofa or in the clothes hamper. As time went on McGuinn also came to sleep on my lap, but only if Melinda was already there—because she likes to sleep with Melinda. All the time and trouble I had taken to bottle-feed McGuinn didn't really seem to matter in the long run.

I got Sally when she was over a year old, when McGuinn was four and Melinda was three. Until I took Sally home she had lived in a cage outdoors and had never been handled. I chose her rather than a young kit because I was looking for something special in markings, color, and body conformation. At that age she was fully developed, so I didn't have to guess at what she would look like later. I found that she was just as easily pan-trained as a kit, even though I was afraid it might be harder because she had lived for so long without ever having seen a pan. She never nipped or bit as some of the kits do, probably because she had already outgrown that stage. She was a little more shy than the average kit, but I believe that if she had been an "only pet" she would have gotten over this much sooner. Being the third ferret in the household, she just didn't get as much attention as the other two did initially.

Since it is really hard to tell much about a kit's personality until you take some time and get to know him, you must basically choose your ferret by sex, color, and just plain intuition.

There isn't really any difference between the male and the female as far as making a good pet goes. The males, however, are twice as big as the females. The average male is about 16 inches long, not counting the tail, and weighs about three pounds, while the female measures about 14 inches and weighs only about a pound and a half. The males also have a broader, less pointed face than the females. With a little experience you can usually sex a kit just by looking at the shape of its face!

If you don't have a size preference and money is a consideration, you might want to choose a male simply because spaying a female usually costs about twice as much as castrating a male, and altering is recommended unless you plan to breed your pet. (See the section on reproduction).

Ferrets come in several colors. The most common is the sable, which has a dark brown coat with a beige undercoat, dark legs and tail, and a dark mask across its eyes. Siamese ferrets have the same markings as the sable, except that their coat is a lighter tan instead of dark brown. White-footed ferrets, sometimes called silver mitts, have white feet or legs and in addition usually have a white bib on the neck. A few have white spots or streaks on the head or back or a white tip on the tail. White-footed ferrets come in various shades ranging from very dark, like the sable, to light tan. They also have a dark mask across the eyes. Silver ferrets have some white mixed in with their dark or tan guard hairs, and the albino ferret is all white and has pink eyes.

If you are buying a kit, don't look for one with a mask, because they don't come that way! Kits begin a mask by growing white hairs in two patches just below the ears, and then the white gradually fills in all across the eyes. Some ferrets have a full mask only when they have a winter coat; in the summer the hair in the middle of the face turns dark again, leaving only the white patches below the ears. A few ferrets have a full mask all year long, but they will still have more white on the face in the winter, which makes their mask appear smaller. McGuinn had a very nice full mask with her first winter coat, but she was spayed the following summer and consequently has never grown another mask. She does, though, get more white across her face in the winter, which gives the faint appearance of a mask.

It also takes time for the guard hairs to grow out on a kit and for the beige undercoat to appear. The older a kit gets the more you will be able to tell about what coloring he will have as an adult.

Regardless of the age, sex, and color you decide on when choosing your kit, you should be sure you are getting a healthy one. He should be alert and active, and his eyes should be bright and clear.

1. This sable white-footed ferret is a female, but her face is much shorter and broader than that of most other female ferrets. **2.** Dr. David Puro occasionally takes his pet ferrets to a park as a change of pace from their normal indoor existence, but his animals are never allowed to roam unsupervised.

2 →

DESCENTING

Unfortunately, many an unsuspecting person has purchased a cuddly baby ferret only to find that as the little fellow grew his odor did too! No one ever told them that when a ferret, especially a male ferret, is fully grown he has a natural body odor that most people find just downright stinky. (A few owners don't mind the strong musky smell, but when given a choice even they readily admit they could do without it!) In such cases what was once a house pet is frequently relegated to life outdoors in a cage out of nose range; worse yet, it's sometimes abandoned entirely.

It happens, unfortunately, that banishing an undescented ferret from the house doesn't solve the odor problem, because when handling an undescented ferret you can count on coming away smelling of ferret. The odor will partially wash off the hands, but it lingers in clothing. Bathing the animal may help temporarily, but in a very short time the ferret will smell like a ferret again, and the only really good solution to this odor problem is descenting.

Much of a ferret's body odor seems to originate in the anal glands, so surgically removing them in much the same manner that a skunk is descented will drastically reduce the odor, provided that the surgically treated ferret is a female. For some reason, probably involving the sex hormones, descenting alone is not adequate for odor control in the male. Descenting helps, but both castration and descenting are needed to eliminate the strong musky smell. If you have a very sensitive nose or take your ferret out to meet people who think that animals should have absolutely NO smell at all, frequent bathing of the descented animal will be necessary to help keep him virtually odor-free.

It is preferable to purchase your ferret from a pet shop or breeder that sells descented and castrated kits. It will be a bit more expensive than an undescented animal, but you will save money in the long run. If you cannot find kits that have already been descented, you don't have to give up the idea of keeping a ferret, because the surgery can be done later by an experienced veterinarian. Most vets who descent skunks will be willing to do it for you. Descenting and castration should both be done at as early an age as possible. Six or seven weeks is the *ideal* age, but a ferret can be descented at *any* age. (No, it's not too late for that two-year-old male you've been keeping out in the garage!)

If you are unable to locate a veterinarian to do the surgery, then you'd be better off purchasing a female, as females have a somewhat milder odor than the males and some people are able to tolerate them undescented if they are given frequent baths.

PREPARING FOR ARRIVAL

In order to be prepared for your new ferret's arrival, you will want to have the following things ready.

A CAGE: Whether or not you will be keeping your ferret caged, when you first bring him home he should be put into a temporary cage or confined to a small area. This is important for several reasons. First, he's going to be in a strange new place, and he will probably be a little frightened. If left loose in a large area, he may hide or get lost. In addition, confining him to a small area is absolutely necessary in order to pan-train him successfully.

The cage can be made out of many different kinds of material, but it is best to avoid using wood if you are building permanent living quarters for your ferret. Wood absorbs odors, and one accident will leave a smell that will encourage your pet to use the same place for a toilet a second time. Wood is also much more difficult to keep clean.

It is important that the cage be large enough to be comfortable and constructed so that your ferret cannot escape. Welded 1" x 1" or 1" x 2" wire is suitable. If you live near a metalwork shop you can have a removable tray with a one-inch lip around the edges made to fit the bottom of the cage. If you design the cage so that this tray slides out easily, you'll make cage cleaning a simple chore.

If you buy a cage, make sure it will hold a ferret! Ferrets can squeeze through deceptively small spaces. It may be a good idea to test the cage with a ferret before making your purchase final.

Even if you do not plan to keep your ferret permanently caged, you will need at least a temporary cage. A large cardboard box like the ones paper towels are shipped in is good for this purpose.

2

1

3

1. Dick Smothers of the comedy/satire Smothers Brothers team treats his ferret Wally to a banana—and Wally doesn't seem to mind sharing with Custer the parrot. 2. Ferrets are easy to travel with, which is why country singer Lacy J. Dalton is able to take her ferret Rona with her when she goes on tour. 3. The sinuousness of the ferret's body—which enables ferrets to be the experts they are at exploring nooks and crannies—is demonstrated in this photo of one of the author's ferrets standing upright; notice how the toes are splayed outward to give the ferret better balance in an unnatural position.

Be prepared to replace it several times, however, because a ferret's cage must be kept clean at all times, and a cardboard box isn't washable!

Some ferrets are unable to jump out of a bathtub, which can be used as a temporary cage. Be sure to keep the bathroom door shut, though, in case your pet learns to jump out while you aren't around! If you have a shower stall with a door that latches firmly you might find the shower a suitable temporary cage.

A BED: A small box or basket is good for this purpose. Some pet stores sell birdhouses which make excellent beds. The entrance hole should be at least two inches in diameter for the female ferret and at least three inches for most full-grown males. Again, wood absorbs odor and is hard to clean, so the disposable cardboard birdhouses are recommended. A small towel or some clean rags can be used for bedding—the bedding should be changed a few times a week and more often if necessary.

FOOD DISH AND WATER BOTTLE: A weighted food dish is best, as it will help prevent a curious kit from overturning it. A hamster or rabbit bottle is recommended for water rather than a bowl, as most young kits and even a few adults enjoy playing with the water and will make a wet mess all over the cage.

LITTER PAN: Almost any type of washable plastic container can serve as a litter pan. It should be at least as tall as the ferret, but not so high that it is difficult to get in and out of.

FERRET-PROOFED ROOMS: Before you bring your ferret home you should thoroughly check every room in which he will be allowed to play. Block up all holes or openings big enough for him to go into. Especially check for openings around the plumbing and heating and air conditioning ducts. Keep in mind that ferrets can actually squeeze *under* some doors! If you'll be letting your ferret into the kitchen, it's a good idea to build some sort of barricade around the stove and refrigerator. Almost all ferrets can get under these appliances and seem to find such niches very comfortable places for napping. Unfortunately, they are potentially dangerous places for your ferret to sleep, and in addition they may be inaccessible to you. If your ferret goes under the stove and you can't reach him, you will just have to wait until he decides to come out!

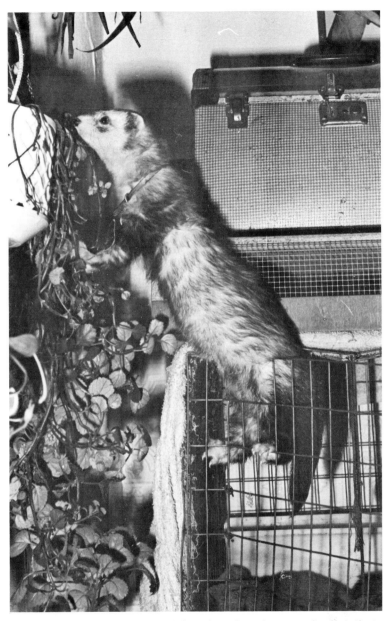

Ferrets are not adept at and fear jumping downwards, but that doesn't stop Daniel, who has discovered that someone forgot to latch his cage door—he'll go up instead!

Ferrets are naturally alert and curious, as can be seen in the photos at left and below, and if they are treated well they will be unafraid and ready to indulge their inquisitiveness.

Handling

Most ferret kits, if they nip or bite, will eventually outgrow it. Some kits never nip at all, while some kits bite—and some bite harder than others. Nipping seems to be an inherited trait, and for this reason it is best to purchase a kit from a pet shop or breeder that sells kits selectively bred for gentleness.

You should not have to wear gloves to handle your new kit any more than you would have to wear them with a new kitten or puppy. If you are getting a ferret that bites hard enough and frequently enough to make wearing gloves necessary you are not getting pet quality stock, and perhaps you should look elsewhere for a pet. This is not to say that you won't get a little nip now and then, but no more than you would expect when handling any new baby animal.

Baby animals nip for several reasons, and ferret babies are no exception. First of all, a very young baby has probably been just recently weaned. It is used to getting milk from its mother and is still learning to eat food from a dish. It takes a while and a little experience before the kit figures out exactly what is food and what is not food. In addition to trying to eat your finger, he is likely to try to eat the dish or spoon as well as the food that is in it. A hungry kit, especially one from a large litter, may have gotten into the habit of competing with littermates for food and will consequently grab or bite something first and then check later (when he's gotten it away from other kits) to see if it's food. You can help by feeding him before you handle him, but even then he may still want to nurse and may try your finger. Fortunately most kits are not too aggressive about this, but it is best to handle them in a manner that will keep your hand out of the range of their tiny teeth.

The best way to pick up a kit is to distract him with one hand while you pick him up with the other. Approaching him from behind, grasp him with your thumb and index finger around his neck, with the other three fingers behind his front legs and under his chest. Then use your other hand to support his rear legs. Never dangle your fingers in front of him, as he is likely to see them as playthings to be attacked and caught. Needless to say, *never* pick up a ferret by his tail!

Baby ferrets may also occasionally nip too hard in playing with you. It may take them a while to learn just how hard they can chomp on your finger without hurting you. After all, until you took them home the only experience they had had in playing and wrestling had probably been with other ferrets who have tough, leathery skin compared to yours. A nip on a littermate's leg may hardly be felt, while a chew of the same magnitude on your finger may hurt! How is the little fellow to know this until you tell him?

He may get the idea if you just screech or holler when he gets too rough. If he chews or hangs on, a little spank on the rear flank will usually cause him to release your finger immediately. After a few times he will probably get the idea and play with you a little more gently. Don't spank him on the head; this will only pound his teeth deeper into your finger. Remember that you are spanking a tiny animal and use the appropriate amount of force—don't beat him to death! Also be sure that the spank occurs while his teeth are actually on you and not afterward when he won't be able to relate the spank to the nip.

Again, it is important to stress that while these nips and bites may be a little painful, they usually won't break the skin and are no more than you would expect from a kitten or puppy. There is a great deal of difference between these nips and the hard bite that consistently draws blood and requires the protection of gloves. Anyone should be able to safely handle a good pet-quality well-fed kit, assuming the handling is done gently and quietly and without frightening the animal.

If you do have a real biter, don't despair. You may have to put up with it for a while, but many, if not most, kits do eventually outgrow the biting habit. If your ferret is six months old or older and still bites and draws blood, he will probably remain a biter. You should try to become aware of the specific situations in which he bites you and try to avoid those situations. Another alternative is to give him to someone who will accept him for the animal he is and will tolerate an occasional bite. Owning this type of animal is a little like owning a wild pet or a nervous dog—you can never totally rely on them not to bite. Again, a ferret is *not* a wild animal and should never be turned loose in the woods. He will be unable to survive and will probably die a painful and unhappy death.

One of the nicest things about owning ferrets is that they are relatively easy to feed. At left and below Daniel and David can be seen enjoying their breakfast.

Feeding Your Ferret

The bulk of your ferret's diet should be a high-quality commercial dry cat chow. This is a nutritionally well-balanced food that will also help keep your pet's teeth strong and healthy. It should be supplemented with canned cat food once every few days because dry cat chow has a very high protein content, and canned food is needed in order to reduce your ferret's protein intake. In addition, fresh water should be available at all times.

Dry chow and canned cat food are all your pet ever needs to eat, but if you wish you may allow him to have some table scraps or special treats occasionally. Ferrets can be given any fruits, vegetables or meat scraps that they will eat. All ferrets have their own peculiar preferences in food. One ferret, for example, may be crazy about blueberries while another might have a weakness

for cucumbers. Like dogs and cats, ferrets should not be allowed to have chicken or turkey bones, which splinter easily.

Almost all ferrets love milk, but they should be allowed to have only a small amount as an infrequent treat, as milk will cause diarrhea. Mixing the milk with an equal amount of water may help to cut down on this problem somewhat.

Ferrets should generally not be allowed to eat sweets, which aren't good for them. A few licks of ice cream once every few months, however, is probably not going to hurt them. If you eat ice cream more often than that, try not to eat it in front of your pet, because all ferrets are wild about ice cream!

Vitamin and mineral supplements should not be necessary if your ferret receives a well-balanced diet of dry chow and canned cat food. If you do give your ferret vitamins, be very careful not to give too much. Almost all pet vitamins and coat conditioners contain vitamin A, which is toxic in large enough doses. Too much vitamin A can, among other things, make your pet's fur fall out. If you are giving your ferret a product that was made for dogs and cats, remember that ferrets are much smaller and should accordingly receive a smaller amount. If you are uncertain about the dosage, consult your veterinarian.

Ferrets have a very high metabolic rate, which means that they use up the food they eat very rapidly. (The ferret's heart beats, on the average, about three times per second!) For this reason it is best to feed your ferret several times a day. Young growing kits should have dry food available to them at all times. In addition they should be given canned food several times a day. A kit that is not being given enough to eat will eat the towel or rags that are being used for his bedding. If you find that your kit has eaten holes in his bedding there is no cause for alarm as this cloth will pass through his digestive system without causing him any great harm—but it certainly won't do him any good either, and the situation should be corrected immediately by making sure that he gets more food!

As your kit gets older, gradually cut the canned food feedings down to once a day and then, if you wish, to once every other day. If—and *only* if—your ferret does not tend to overeat once he is fully grown, you can continue to leave dry food in his dish at all times. If he begins to gain weight you will have to restrict his food intake by feeding him a small amount twice a day and by not leaving any food out for him at other times.

Most ferret kits are neither too fat nor too thin, so watch to see that your pet keeps the nice slim and trim figure he had when you got him, and feed him accordingly. Being overweight is bad for *all* animals, and a fat ferret is likely to be less active and have more health problems than a normal ferret. In addition he will have a significantly shorter life span.

Ferrets like to "cache" things, and their food is no exception. When they finish eating they will frequently carry away bits of food in their mouth to store in their bed, under the furniture, or in some other favorite hiding place. A very industrious ferret will make numerous such trips until the bowl is completely empty and the entire remains of his dinner have been safely put away. Many ferrets, if offered a tidbit of food that doesn't appeal to their taste, will nevertheless accept the offering—only to carry it off, hide it, and then come back to get more!

Because of this tendency to relocate leftovers, moist or canned food should be removed as soon as your ferret has finished eating. This way you can avoid having spoiled food under your sofa! If dry food is left out all of the time, many ferrets eventually lose interest in moving it around. If the transportation of dry food is a problem, though, you may have to feed your ferret in a restricted area in which you can control such behavior. Otherwise you may have to stop leaving out dry food.

There is absolutely no reason whatsoever to feed your ferret mice, birds, toads, frogs, or any other kind of small animal either dead or alive! These animals will more than likely be infested with external parasites in addition to any number of internal parasites that can make your ferret very sick. White mice that can be purchased at a pet store will, of course, be free of these parasites. Dogs, cats, and ferrets are all carnivorous animals, and if you believe in buying mice to feed your dog or cat, then you might want to do the same for your ferret. To do so, however, will NOT improve your ferret's diet and will serve absolutely NO purpose whatsoever! Most ferrets who have grown up eating cat chow will not even recognize live animals as food anyway.

A sturdy, roomy cage as shown at left and below is a very handy ferret-connected item to have available, even if you do not plan to keep your ferret permanently confined to it—and a cage is almost a necessity if you plan to train a ferret to use a litter pan.

Housebreaking

Ferrets are instinctively clean and very much creatures of habit. In addition, they like to use a corner for their toilet. For these reasons, ferrets can be easily trained to use a litter pan. Since pans have nice corners, all you really have to do is to help your ferret get into the habit of using the corner you have chosen for him—the one in his pan!

Whether or not you will be keeping your ferret in a cage, when you first bring him home he should be put in a temporary cage or confined to a small area. This is absolutely essential if you wish to pan-train him.

Set up his area with a pan in one corner. You can use a cat litter pan which is available at pet shops, a small plastic dish pan, or even a plastic container such as the type that is used for stor-

ing food. If your ferret is very young you may wish to cut one side of the pan down a few inches (especially if you are using a plastic dish pan) to make it easier for him to climb into.

It is also important that he have a box or basket that he can use for a bed. Otherwise he may want to sleep in his litter pan.

Either clay cat litter material or the green-type litter can be used in the pan. The green litter works especially well because it is more absorbent and effective at deodorizing than conventional litter and is made up of small pellets that don't stick to the paws and track outside the pan as clay litter sometimes does.

Newspaper or paper towels can also be used, but they are less desirable because they must be changed quite frequently and are not very absorbent. In addition, they do not help to control odor. Another drawback of newspaper is that in using it the ferret is likely to get his feet wet, and this contributes to the odor problem. Basically the only time newspaper is advantageous is for the ferret who has free run of the house and has chosen his own corner. Usually in such cases the ferret has trained his owner to put newspaper down for him—often because he has chosen an inconvenient corner for a pan or because a pan won't fit. If you use newspaper and find that your ferret gets the walls dirty, you can tape the newspaper two or three inches up the wall, which should solve the problem quite nicely.

Start the housebreaking procedure by putting a small amount of litter in the pan along with some of your kit's feces and thoroughly mixing the two together. This is necessary, because if you don't do it, all you've really done is to make your kit a nice sandbox in which to play. He will delight in digging, rooting with his nose and generally scattering litter all over the place! It's lots of fun for him but a big mess for you to clean up. Also, he won't want to use such a nice play area for a toilet and will most likely pick another spot for this purpose.

The secret to getting him to use the pan is to make it an undesirable place to play. Ferrets are clean animals, and even the friskiest, most playful kit won't want to play in a dirty litter pan. At the same time it is important to keep the rest of his cage or area *spotless*. This may mean that you will have to clean his area two or three times a day for the first few days, but he'll soon catch on.

40

Until your kit gets older you'll probably find it unwise to completely clean out the litter pan, even if your kit is very good about using it. Take out some of the most soiled litter and put in a little fresh litter on top instead of changing it entirely. As time goes by you can make the pan cleaner and cleaner until finally, when your ferret is an adult, you should be able to use 100% fresh litter when desired with no problem at all.

If you use newspaper in the pan you may find that the kits enjoy taking the newspaper out and tearing it up into little pieces. To avoid having to leave the paper too dirty while at the same time discouraging the kits from playing in it, you can add a very small amount of water, which often makes it less inviting—but needless to say, also less absorbent!

Another problem you may have with the pan is that kits sometimes enjoy moving it around to different locations in the cage; they may even turn it upside down. In this case you may want to weight it down or tie it into place. In addition, I find that giving them other toys and other objects to look at and play with will often distract their attention from the litter pan and curtail such behavior. Give them a clothes pin, a shoe box with a hole cut in it, a bottle cap, or almost any other household object that can serve as a safe toy. Just remember to change objects frequently, because each object will hold a kit's attention for only a limited amount of time.

While your ferret is confined to his cage or small area, you should have no problem in getting him to use the pan. If after several days he is still not using the pan consistently, decrease the size of his area until he does use it. Although it is very rarely necessary, especially with a kit, as a last resort you will be able to get him to use the pan by arranging it so that he has an area so small that he literally has to choose between using his bed for a toilet and using his pan for a toilet. Once he is using the pan consistently, gradually increase his living space again.

Your ferret should continue to live in a confined area for at least a month and possibly for several months so that his habit of using the pan will become firmly established. When he is out of his living quarters you should be with him and should always have a litter pan available nearby. Keep a close eye on him to make sure he doesn't eliminate anywhere but in the pan. Be sure

David has just used his litter pan and waits to be taken out of his cage.

to put him into the pan after he wakes up from a nap and shortly after he eats. If you do catch him in the act of going to the toilet elsewhere, pick him up immediately and put him into his pan. Watch for any signs of restlessness such as running around in circles, running from corner to corner, or backing up into the corner, as these actions usually mean that it is time to use the pan again.

If you are planning to eventually let your ferret have free run of the house or apartment, you should increase his living area gradually. After he has been in his temporary cage at least a month and has been good about using the pan, you can try confining him to a small room, such as the bathroom, instead. Gradually increase the size and number of rooms he is allowed to be in. Use the same technique as before. Decrease the area when he isn't using the pan and continue to increase the area as long as he is using it.

As his area begins to include several rooms it is a good idea to put down two or more litter pans, possibly in corners he has chosen himself. Many ferrets will not bother to go back to a pan if it is too far away and instead will find a closer spot.

Ferrets are intelligent, and by the time they reach adulthood they will know that they are supposed to use the litter pan or newspaper if they have been properly trained. In a cage you should have no problem with any ferret. Some ferrets are more easily pan-trained than others, and occasionally you will find a ferret that, no matter what you do to encourage him, will just not use the pan when given free run of the house. In this case (unless you are willing to tolerate cleaning up after your pet) it is best to make a small area or cage his permanent home and allow him to come out and play for a while each day—*after* he has used the litter pan in his cage. While this may not seem like an ideal situation for the ferret, it is better for him than becoming an abandoned pet. Most ferrets adapt very well to such a living situation and appear to be quite happy as long as they are let out to play for a while each day.

It is important to note that a ferret given free run of the house may, like a cat, stop using the pan when it gets too dirty or when he is upset or frightened or after an undesirable change in his daily routine.

Left: Melinda being soaped gently but thoroughly during her bath. *Below:* Looking a little crestfallen but not absolutely miserable (Melinda and the author's other ferrets have become accustomed to the bath routine over the course of time), she patiently awaits the next step in the process.

Ferret Grooming

Although bathing your ferret is not a necessity, an occasional bath will help keep your pet odor-free. In addition it will make his coat look fluffy and full. While most ferrets usually are not too enthusiastic about a bath and see it as something that must be tolerated, some ferrets actually learn to enjoy it.

The quickest and easiest way to bathe a ferret is to hold him under the tap in the kitchen sink. Make sure that the water is not too hot or too cold. When he is entirely wet, lather him from head to toe with a mild "tear-free" baby shampoo. Tear-free shampoo will enable you to wash the entire head including the face—and the head seems to be one of the places where odor builds up the most!

Melinda and McGuinn find that the one redeeming aspect of a bath is the baby shampoo, which they like to eat, and they happily lick the lather off themselves and my hands. (Although I find all soap totally unpalatable, many ferrets find it quite tasty and actually enjoy snacking on a bar of soap—which should be discouraged because, although it is generally harmless, it is of doubtful nutritional value!)

1. Melinda gets rinsed with the sink spray attachment while (2) McGuinn, McKendree and Sally enjoy a pre-bath frolic.

1

1. Melinda gets a
good shampoo and
then (2) goes for a
swim—to the nearest
shore!

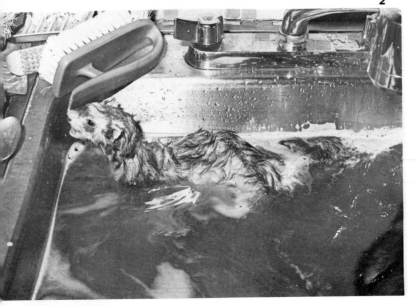
2

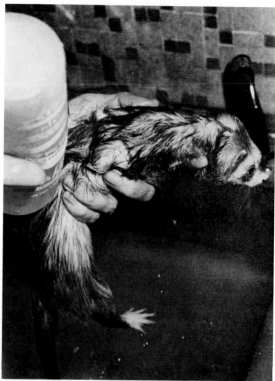

1. Melinda has her fur checked to make sure that it's soap-free after her rinse, and then (2) she takes time out to sample the taste of a bar of soap.

After a good lathering, rinse well by holding your pet under the faucet again. Be sure to include the face, taking care not to get water up the nose. After removing excess water, give your ferret a towel and he will dry himself off! Don't put the towel on the floor, however, or turn him loose in the house, as he will use other things in addition to the towel to dry off with and he may end up dirtier than he was when you started! The bathtub and a clean bed (either his or yours) are both good places for him to get dry. Be sure that the house is warm and draft-free so he won't get a chill and catch cold. Now stand back and watch your pet jump around and play! Most ferrets are especially frisky after a bath!

If you want to take more time in giving your ferret a bath, you can fill the bathtub with four or five inches of water and let him do a little swimming while you're at it. All ferrets are good swimmers, but even though a few have been reported to enjoy swimming, most ferrets will swim only to keep from drowning and will quickly head for the closest shore! McGuinn, although she never gets in voluntarily, does appear to enjoy a leisurely soak in warm water if it is not very deep and she is able to touch the bottom.

Most ferrets can be bathed as often as once every week or ten days without drying out their skin.

Ferrets have wash and wear coats which never need brushing or combing—in fact most ferrets hate to be brushed and will not sit still for it. Occasionally a ferret will do a little grooming on his own, much like a cat does. McGuinn frequently washes her feet, and all of my ferrets will wash their face once in a while.

Ferrets should have their claws trimmed frequently. They do not have needle-sharp claws like those of cats, but because their claws are so small the ends may get sharp enough to scratch you. Trimming is most easily done with a fingernail clipper. Look for the blood vein in the claw and be sure not to cut it. To do so will make the claw bleed and will also cause pain. If you are uncertain about how far back to cut, your veterinarian can show you.

Most ferrets hate to have their claws trimmed and will not hold still while you do it. You may find it is easier to have someone else hold your pet while you clip. Another method which I use is to sneak up on them while they are asleep. I can sometimes get two or three nails cut before it wakes them up!

1. Melinda licking soap off the author's hand and (2) deciding she's had enough and climbing out of the sink.

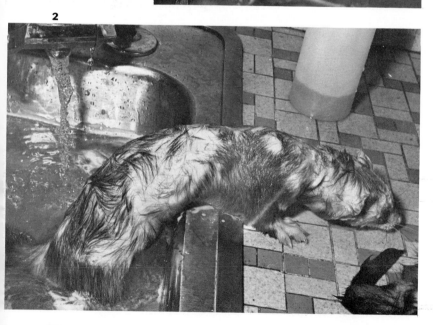

1

First Melinda (1) and then both Melinda and other of the author's ferrets (2) that have been bathed during the session snuggle up in toweling material to get dry.

2

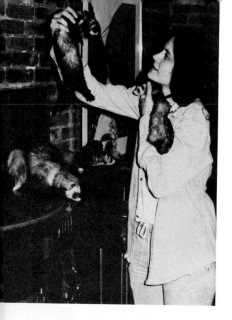

All of the ferrets shown at left and below are obviously frisky and healthy. To insure their continued good health they have been vaccinated against both feline and canine distemper.

Ferret Health

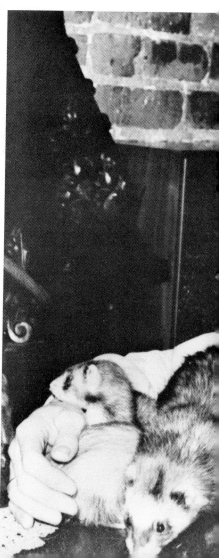

Ferrets are susceptible to both feline and canine distemper and should be vaccinated yearly against both diseases. This is very important because distemper is always fatal to ferrets. They can be protected against canine distemper by vaccination with a modified live virus of chicken embryo tissue culture. Vaccine prepared from ferret cell culture should not be used because the attenuated virus may retain its virulence for its natural host and can cause distemper in your ferret rather than preventing it. Ferrets should be inoculated against feline distemper with killed

tissue vaccines only. Live or modified live vaccines should not be used as they may cause feline distemper in your pet.

If you are living in an area where vaccinating cats against rabies is recommended, then you may want to vaccinate your ferret. This will probably be unnecessary however, because it is unlikely that your ferret will be exposed to rabies. Your veterinarian will be able to advise you on this matter. When vaccinating against rabies it is EXTREMELY IMPORTANT to use KILLED TISSUE VACCINE. Live or modified live vaccine can give your ferret rabies. This is very serious not only because it would kill your ferret, but also because your pet can transmit rabies to you, and rabies is also fatal to human beings. Rabies vaccine should not be given before six months of age.

It is advisable to check with your veterinarian a few months before your ferret's booster shots are due so that if he does not keep the proper vaccines on hand he will be able to order them for you.

Ferrets tend to scratch themselves frequently. This is normal and should not be taken as a sign that they have fleas unless they have been in a flea-infested area or have been around other animals that have fleas. You can check for fleas by gently blowing on your pet, which will part his fur and enable you to see the skin where fleas may be crawling around. Little specks of black "dirt" near the skin may also be a sign of fleas. If you are in doubt about whether or not your animal has fleas, consult your veterinarian. If your pet does have them, a cat flea collar or spray containing pyrethrins may be used safely.

Excessive scratching may also indicate dry skin, especially if your ferret is living in a radiator-heated room where the air is very dry. A humidifier to moisten the air is the best solution to this problem, but a small amount of butter, oil, or mayonnaise added to the food may also help to alleviate this condition.

Ferrets can get ear mites. Frequent shaking of the head or scratching of the ears can be a sign of these parasites, which will cause your pet's ears to look dirty. This condition should be treated by a veterinarian immediately, as left untreated it can cause ear infection and even deafness. If your pet is bothered by a build-up of earwax, you should have your veterinarian show you how to clean his ears safely and without puncturing the ear drum.

Female ferrets left in heat for long periods of time frequently develop an infection of the uterus which is usually fatal. To avoid this do not allow your ferret to remain in heat. (See the later section about ferret reproductive systems.)

There are several types of parasitic worms and protozoans that will affect ferrets. In order to make sure that your animal is free of such parasites, it is advisable to have your veterinarian examine a fecal sample several times a year.

If your ferret has diarrhea it could be due to something he has eaten. Withhold solid food for 12 hours and cut any milk or meat out of his diet for a few days, and the problem should correct itself. If the diarrhea lasts longer than a few days or if your pet appears ill, you should take him to the doctor, as it could be a sign of parasites or some serious problem.

If your ferret sneezes it may mean that he has a cold. Ferrets are susceptible to the common cold and may catch yours if exposed to it. As in humans, this condition is not serious. Ferrets will have the same symptoms as people do: runny nose, sneezing, and fever. They should be kept warm and dry and be encouraged to rest. Ferrets can also get various other upper respiratory diseases, so if your pet appears sick and refuses food you should take him to the veterinarian for treatment.

Sneezing does not necessarily mean that your ferret is sick. If he has been running around under the bed or other furniture that isn't dusted under frequently, it could very well be that he has just gotten dust up his nose!

The first signs of a sick ferret are often lethargy and a decrease in appetite. If your ferret skips more than two or three meals, it is advisable to take him to a veterinarian right away. Early detection and treatment of an illness may save his life!

FERRET SAFETY

Because of their small size, unusual appearance, and natural tendency to burrow, pet ferrets are subject to numerous safety hazards, especially if they are allowed free run of the house.

One major danger is that ferrets are easily stepped on. They are so small and silent that you don't usually hear them approach, and if you aren't very careful to look before you step you may accidentally injure your pet. My ferrets are continually underfoot as they follow me around the house, and even with little warning bells on their collars they end up getting a toe stepped on now and then—to which they respond vocally with what sounds a bit like cursing in Chinese!

Because ferrets love to burrow they will frequently crawl under a rug, the corner of a blanket, or an article of clothing left on the floor. It may turn out to be a disaster for your little critter if you walk on something he is napping in or under!

Reclining chairs and convertible sofa beds are also potential dangers for the ferret who crawls underneath or inside them for a nap. Unfortunately I know of several such pets who were crushed to death by an unsuspecting owner.

Some ferrets like to crawl into or underneath the washing machine or dryer or like to sleep in a pile of dirty clothes. These places should be off limits to your pet, but care should be taken not to wash, dry, or otherwise injure him in case he trespasses occasionally.

Several ferrets have been known to crawl unnoticed into the refrigerator, and although they did make enough noise to alert their owners, they also made quite a mess!

Another ever-present danger for the pet ferret is the ignorance of neighbors. Most people don't have any idea of what a ferret is. If your pet happens to slip out the door or otherwise get out of your house or apartment, he may be unlucky enough to encounter someone who thinks he is a rat and get beaten to death with a broomstick.

To help protect your ferret against all of these dangers, it is a good idea to have your pet wear a collar with an identification tag and a small bell. He may not like the idea at first, but after 10 or 15 minutes it won't bother him any more and he will be much safer. The collar will indicate that *whatever* it is it must be someone's pet, so hopefully he won't be killed by the first terrified person he tries to make friends with. Also, the identification tag may help get him returned to you—if anyone is brave enough to pick him up and read it! The bell will serve as a locator to tell you when he's underfoot so that you can avoid stepping on him. It will also let you hear him slip out the door when you might not have seen him.

The collar should be reasonably thin and lightweight; a kitten collar cut down to a smaller size works well and can be purchased at any pet store. (Perhaps as ferrets become more popular pet stores will even begin to sell *ferret* collars!) Your pet's collar should be tight enough that it does not easily slip off over his head but loose enough that you can get your little finger underneath it. You will probably have to punch extra holes in the collar in order to be able to adjust it properly. Remember to check a growing animal frequently to make sure the collar has not become too snug. Even a small weight gain in an adult animal can cause a collar to be too tight. Be sure to have a spare collar and be prepared to replace lost collars several times a year, as most ferrets seem to manage to slip out of and lose collars occasionally.

I suppose there is always some danger that a ferret may get hung up somewhere by his collar, but I feel that the dangers of not wearing a collar are much greater. Thus far I know of many ferret owners who have had their pet saved or returned because of the collar, but I don't know of a single ferret that has yet had any problems *caused* by its collar!

Your ferret should not be allowed to run free outdoors unless you are watching him at all times. Once ferrets have gotten used to other animals they will not be afraid, and they'll have no protection against a vicious dog or any other predator. In addition, while at first they will probably stay close to the house, they may eventually wander off and may easily get into trouble or get lost. If you are playing with your ferret in the park or in your yard, you may want to attach a leash to his collar and let him drag it around behind him. It will be useful for stopping him quickly when a strange dog approaches (or he approaches a strange dog) or when he starts to disappear down a hole you hadn't noticed.

Ferrets readily form friendships with other animals and will wrestle and play "chase" with dogs, cats, and sometimes even skunks and rabbits. You should take care, however, when introducing them to new animals, because one bite from an unfriendly dog or cat could mean instant death for your little pet.

Left and below:
Melinda nursing her
first litter of kits.

*Ferret
Reproductive
Systems*

Reproduction is a somewhat complex subject, but taking the time to understand the fascinating chain of events that occurs during ferret reproduction can be rewarding and well worth the effort. The ferret is especially interesting because its reproductive cycle is different from that of a dog or a cat, but most importantly the knowledge of how the reproductive system functions will enable you to take the simple precautions that are necessary to keep your pet ferret, particularly your female ferret, in good health.

Ferrets are seasonal breeders—that is, they reproduce only during a specific time of the year when living in a natural environment. It is likely that this system evolved as a protective measure to ensure that the young would be born only in the spring and

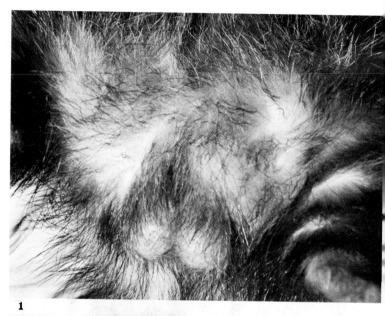

1

2

Closeups of genitalia of male and female ferrets. 1. This ferret is beginning to go into season, so his testicles are easily visible. 2. Because this female is not in heat, her vulva is not noticeable. 3. This female's vulva may become even more swollen when she is fully in heat. 4. This female has been bred, so her vulva has gone down somewhat in size. It will remain at about the size shown until after her kits are born.

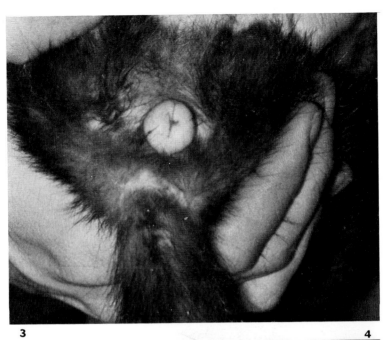

3

4

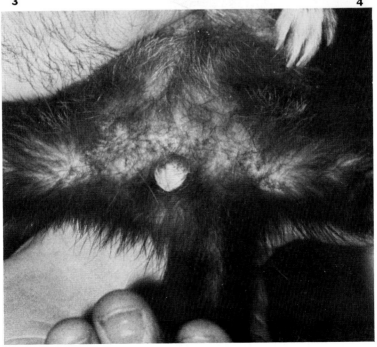

61

summer when the weather is warmer and food and water are more readily accessible, thus increasing their chances of survival.

The female is receptive to a mate only when she is in estrus or heat. At other times she will refuse the advances of a male and is not capable of becoming pregnant. The male, like the female, is not sexually active all year. If presented with a female in heat before he has come into season, the male will make no sexual advances. In addition, he is not producing viable sperm at this time and is incapable of impregnating the female.

This yearly cycle of sexual activity and inactivity is regulated by light/dark conditions. As the spring approaches the days increase in length and the nights become shorter. This change in day length is perceived by the retina of the ferret's eye and signals are transmitted to the brain. The brain then sends the messages on to the pituitary gland, which is also located in the head. The pituitary gland responds to this message by secreting a hormone known as "follicle stimulating hormone", also known as FSH. The FSH travels through the ferret's blood stream and acts on the reproductive organs, causing them, in turn, to secrete the sex hormones which cause the ferret to become sexually active.

Using day length to control the readiness of the ferret to reproduce is a very good system, because if another indicator such as temperature were used to signal the impending spring, unseasonably warm or cold days could easily lead these animals astray and disrupt the timing, causing the young to be born too early or too late. It has been shown in various studies that temperature has no effect on the reproductive cycle and neither does the gradual increase in day length. Rather it is the intensity, wavelength, and duration of the light itself that affects the cycle, as well as the duration of the dark period. Ferrets shed only two times a year, once to change from summer to winter coat and another time to change from winter to summer coat. These coat changes are closely associated with the reproductive cycle and are also controlled by the light/dark conditions.

THE FEMALE

In the female, numerous changes begin to occur at the onset of estrus or heat. FSH released from the pituitary causes the eggs or ova, which are produced in follicles within the ovaries, to ripen in preparation for release into the uterus. FSH, along with small amounts of another pituitary hormone known as "lutenizing hormone" or LH, stimulates the ovaries to produce and release the sex hormone estrogen. Estrogen in turn brings about changes in both the internal and external reproductive organs. It causes enlargement of the uterus as a whole and in particular causes an increase in the depth of the mucosal lining of the uterus. There is a marked increase in the number of blood vessels supplying the uterus and, in addition, mucus-secreting glands develop.

Externally, there is a swelling of the vulva, which continues until the vulva is about 50 times its normal size. A serous fluid is secreted, often in sufficient quantity to wet the entire underside of the hind legs, lower abdomen, and anal/tail area. There is a generalized increase in body odor, even if the ferret has been descented. The undescented ferret in estrus, however, will have a much stronger smell than the descented one.

Behaviorally, estrus has very little effect on the female, other than to cause her to be receptive to a male ferret. She may become a little more active than usual, but most likely the fact that she is in heat would go unnoticed if it weren't for her obvious large, turgid vulva. (This will probably be appreciated by anyone who has survived one or more heat periods of a Siamese cat or any other talkative cat!)

If the female is bred, copulation will stimulate the pituitary gland to put out its hormones in different amounts. FSH secretion is greatly decreased, and a large amount of LH is suddenly released into the blood stream. LH acts on the follicles of the ovaries to cause ovulation, which is the release of the ova or eggs. The shed ova move down the fallopian tubes, where they can be fertilized by sperm from the male. They subsequently divide and become embedded in the uterus, where they develop into fetuses. After about 42 days, plus or minus one day, the young are born.

A few days after ovulation has been induced by mating, hormonal changes will cause the vulva to begin to decrease in size. If mating does not take place, the female will remain in heat throughout the entire breeding season, which extends from the latter part of March through July or August, and the vulva will remain in its swollen condition. While enlargement of the vulva no doubt makes the mating process easier for the male and thus increases the chances for the female to conceive, it also presents a dangerous problem for the female who is not bred and who consequently remains in heat. The enlarged opening provides an excellent avenue for the introduction of infection. In addition, the built up mucosal lining of the uterus provides a good nutrient for the growth of bacteria and other infecting organisms. For these reasons a female who is allowed to remain in heat for any length of time is at risk for the development of endometritis or a pyometra, both serious uterine infections. Unfortunately these infections are usually fatal in the ferret, because by the time the symptoms are noticed the infection has progressed too far to be treated successfully. The seriousness of this condition is probably exacerbated by the fact that ferrets in heat will show a gradual weight loss, so that the longer they have been in heat before they become infected the worse general condition they are in and the less able they are to fight off the infection.

Most owners don't realize their pet is sick until she stops eating and becomes very listless, depressed, and apathetic. Other symptoms include anemia (the gums and paw pads will appear pale or almost white instead of a nice healthy pink), dehydration, and fever. If the fever is very high the nose will feel dry and hot to the touch. This temperature increase is eventually followed by a rapid and drastic decrease in temperature which closely precedes death.

Once any of these symptoms are obvious in a ferret that is in heat, she should be taken to a veterinarian without delay. The treatment is to administer antibiotics, rehydrate, and force feed. (If you notice that she is lethargic and get her in for medical attention *before* she stops eating, her chances for survival are much better.) Ideally she should have emergency surgery and be spayed, which might (but will not always) save her life. Usually by the time a sick ferret is taken to the veterinarian her condition is so bad that she would not be able to survive the trauma of surgery. In this case most vets will try to stabilize her condition in hopes of doing the surgery when she is better. Unfortunately I have not yet heard of even one ferret who was too sick for surgery who improved enough to be operated on. Even such drastic measures as blood transfusions don't seem to do any good. They all invariably die.

Just how likely it is that a female left in heat will develop an infection is difficult to say. No controlled studies have been done to determine the percentage of females likely to have this problem. Even if there were such a study it would not tell you whether your ferret would be in the group to live or the group to die. If you leave your ferret in heat, the odds are probably not in her favor, and while she might survive the first few breeding seasons (and then again she might not), it is doubtful that she will die of old age. This infection, in fact, is probably currently the leading cause of death in unaltered female pet ferrets. If you care about your pet and want her to live out her full life span of ten or 12 years, you most certainly won't want to play Russian roulette with her life and will not allow her to remain in heat.

If you don't want to let your female have kits, the ideal solution to the problem of prolonged estrus is to have her spayed. Then she won't go into heat at all and you can avoid the problem entirely. Another advantage to spaying is that neutered females have a little less odor than the unaltered females, even in the winter when the unaltered females are not in heat. There is no noticeable change in the behavior or personality of a spayed female, and the only difference you'll find between the two is that the altered female may not grow quite as thick a winter coat and in some cases won't show quite as much color change in going from a summer to a winter coat as does the unaltered female.

If you want your pet to have kits at some time and consequently don't want to spay her (and this should be the *only* reason for not spaying her!), then she should be brought out of heat with hormones each time you wish to skip breeding her.

An injection of 100 USP units of chorionic gonadatropin, which acts like LH to promote ovulation, can be used for this purpose. The first injection should be given after the vulva reaches full size, usually about two weeks after you first begin to notice the swelling. If this hormone has induced ovulation, which will terminate estrus, the vulva should begin to decrease in size within about a week and continue to get smaller. If after this time the vulva shows no signs of going down, a second dose

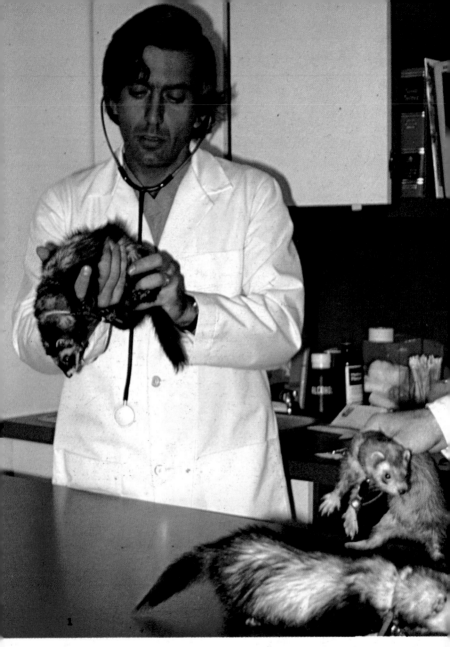

A group of ferrets during their visit to the veterinarian. In (1) Melinda is about to get a hormone shot to bring her safely out of heat. In (2) Sally is having her claws trimmed by the veterinarian.

2 →

should be given. If there is no sign of regression the following week, a third dose of 200 USP units should be given.

If chorionic gonadatropin is unavailable, Ovaban, a cat birth control pill, can be given instead. The initial dose is 10 mg; use 20 mg if a later dose is necessary. Of course the aid of a veterinarian is essential in obtaining and giving these hormones.

If two or three doses of hormone have been given and your ferret shows no signs of going out of heat (which can and does happen), then I strongly recommend that you stop playing around with hormones and find a male ferret to do the job of terminating your pet's estrous condition. This is a fool-proof method as long as the male you are using is mature and sexually active. Although it may result in pregnancy, it is preferable to the continued risk of infection and death.

If a male is unavailable another solution is to spay her, but this is a less desirable solution (especially if you wanted to breed her in the future) because while she is in heat the increased blood supply to the enlarged uterus increases the risk of hemorrhage and other surgical complications.

While your female is in heat you should monitor her condition especially carefully. If you have several ferrets sharing the same food dish and you don't take note of the activity level of each one, then you may have a very sick female before you realize that the other animals were eating her food and it wasn't just a coincidence that she was napping the last several times you observed her.

Checking the condition of each ferret frequently when several are kept together is a good general practice whether or not your female is in heat. This includes making sure that each animal eats at feeding time. This may be more difficult if you leave dry food out all of the time, but it is important because knowing that your pet is not eating may alert you to a problem at an early stage when it can still be treated successfully.

THE MALE

In the male the release of FSH from the pituitary gland stimulates the growth of Sertoli cells in the testicles. The Sertoli cells protect, nourish, and permit the growth of sperm cells. LH causes the testis to secrete the male sex hormone testosterone. Until the level of testosterone in the bloodstream has reached a high enough level, the male will show no sexual interest in the female. When testosterone levels rise sufficiently the male begins to show sexual behavior such as mounting of the female. While testosterone levels may be high enough to cause mating, they must be even higher in order for mature sperm to be produced, so it is possible for the male to have enough testosterone to cause mating before there is enough to cause the production of mature sperm. At this stage sterile mating can occur, which will still cause the female to ovulate and will bring her out of heat. She will not, however, conceive and become pregnant.

It is not quite as easy to tell if a male has come into season as it is with the female. In the winter period of sexual inactivity the testes are small, soft, and in a forward position in the groin. As the male begins to come into season the testes move back and into a position in the scrotum just in front of the anus. At the same time the testes begin to enlarge and become turgid. The hair will appear thinned out over the testes until, at the time of greatest testis size, the scrotum will be almost bare.

When the male begins to go out of season, testosterone levels gradually fall and sperm production ceases before mating activity, which can again result in sterile matings.

If you are not going to use your male for breeding it is best to have him castrated. There are several reasons for this, but perhaps the most compelling one is odor. Male ferrets that have not been castrated (including descented ones) have a very strong odor, and most people find they can't keep an unaltered male indoors as a house pet. (I keep my studs in a cage out the kitchen window of my apartment!) In addition to the unpleasant odor, uncastrated males have several undesirable habits such as urinating in little "spots" all over the house. A sexually active male will mount and bite the neck of a female even if she is not in heat and will "bother" other males in the same manner. Two males who were not kept together while they came into season will fight and injure one another when put together.

Because there are so many problems associated with keeping a stud ferret, you are better off seeking stud service for your female if you wish to breed her.

Left: Baby ferrets shown at an age of a little over two weeks. *Below:* A mother ferret nursing her kits.

Breeding
And
Birth

MATING

Many pet ferrets who live indoors are subjected to electric light after sundown, which has the effect of increasing the length of their day. Because day length controls the cycle of sexual activity and inactivity in the ferret, these artificially long days can cause both the male and the female to come into season at any time of the year. Pet females, however, should not be bred more than once a year, because the physical stress of having two or three litters a year may shorten their life-span. Pregnancy makes demands on the body of a female ferret, just as it does on the body of any other female mammal, throughout the gestation period and at the moment of birth. The nursing process also makes demands on the mother's body.

There are individual differences in the response of each ferret to light, so several animals living under the same lighting conditions may go into season weeks or even months apart and may come out of season at different times as well. For this reason male and female sexual activity levels frequently do not coincide during the winter or early and late in the natural breeding season, and the chances of having a successful mating resulting in pregnancy are best from about April through the middle of July.

Ferrets in a natural environment become sexually mature the first spring following their birth, when they are about a year old. Ferrets born in the winter or ferrets kept under electric lighting, however, may experience accelerated maturation and become capable of reproducing at as young an age as four or five months.

Females should be bred when the vulva has reached its maximum size, which usually occurs about two weeks after the swelling is first noticeable. The only *sure* ways of knowing whether a sexually active male is fully in season and producing sperm in sufficient numbers to impregnate a female is to look at his semen under a microscope, although the increased size and rearward position of his testes will give some indication.

Courtship of a female in full estrus by a potent male is very rough and even violent at times. Although it may look to you as if the female is in danger of being killed, the courtship is normal for ferrets and not anything to worry about!

Using his teeth, the male grasps the female by the nape of the neck, sometimes even breaking the skin. The female becomes almost passive while the male throws her back and forth and drags her about on the ground. In time she becomes more and more submissive. When she is almost completely limp the male, still gripping her by the back of the neck, throws her on her side and holds her in place with his front legs and partially with his hind legs while he attempts entry, which may take anywhere from several minutes to half an hour.

After successful entry and copulation the animals may remain locked in position for as long as three hours. On separation the male may be left with the female or removed. If they are left together further matings will likely occur.

One successful copulation will induce ovulation in the female, and if the male was fertile pregnancy may result. If the male is not yet fully in season and a sterile mating occurs, the female will nevertheless ovulate and a pseudo-pregnancy, or false pregnancy, will be the result. In addition, ovulation induced by hormones may also cause a false pregnancy. Both false pregnancy and true pregnancy show the same signs, including enlargement of the abdomen and mammary glands, and it is difficult to tell the difference between these two conditions until about three weeks after the mating, when an experienced veterinarian will be able to feel the fetuses growing within the uterus.

THE PREGNANT FEMALE

After you breed your female you should care for her as if she were pregnant, even though it may be quite a while before you know for sure whether or not the mating was successful.

Your ferret will have an increased appetite at this time and should be allowed to eat as much as she wishes. She will also probably want to sleep a lot more; this is normal.

Although the vulva will decrease in size significantly, it will still remain a little swollen, and there may even be a thick clear mucous discharge from the vagina; this discharge is nothing to worry about.

About three or four weeks after ovulation is induced (whether by hormones or breeding) the female will begin to shed her winter coat. She may do this slowly over a long period of time, or it may come out all at once by the handful. Sometimes the new summer coat growth can be seen close to the skin under the old winter coat. In some ferrets, however, the new coat does not begin to grow out until much later, leaving them with a thin, scraggly appearance. Sometimes when this happens parts of the feet and legs and other areas around the eyes, nose, and mouth become almost bald and may remain that way for some time. I have gotten more than one call from the worried owner of such a ferret who was afraid his pet had some terrible skin disease! Although it may look very bad, it is just a part of a normal coat change, so just be patient and the new summer coat will eventually grow in.

1. With their eyes not yet opened, these baby ferrets are huddled together in their nest for warmth. 2. A mother ferret carrying one of her babies back to the nest.

The pregnant female ferret can, for the most part, pretty much go on with life as usual until a few days before the kits are due. (Although Sally, Melinda, and McGuinn didn't work, they did go to school with me right up until the day their babies were born!) If your pet has free run of the house, however, it is a good idea to confine her to a cage or a small area during the last two weeks of her pregnancy and until the kits are weaned. If left unconfined, she may, like a cat, hide her kits or move them about from place to place. This is not good, because you need to be able to check on both mother and kits frequently to be sure that all is well. In addition your pet may choose somewhere totally unreasonable to keep her kits. I woke up in the middle of the night more than once to find that Melinda had moved her entire family into bed with me before I finally realized that she was not going to give up and take no for an answer. The only solution to this problem was to lock her up!

You should put your pet into her cage or small area several weeks before the kits are born, because if you wait until the kits are due to confine her, she may become so upset that she will ignore her new kits entirely and concentrate on regaining her freedom. If she is confined progressively more each day, by the time the kits arrive she will be accustomed to the restriction and can turn her attention to her babies.

Her cage or area should contain a bed or "nest" for her to keep her kits in. An ordinary cardboard box is fine if you cut down one side a little so she won't overturn it when climbing in and out. A clean towel can be used for bedding—it should be large enough for your pet to cover herself and her kits with, but not so large that the kits will get lost in it.

As the due date for the birth of the kits draws near, both the pregnant and the pseudo-pregnant female may look and act pregnant. Some females become overly affectionate and may lick your hands or face incessantly, almost as if they are practicing their mothering skills on you. During the sixth and last week of a true pregnancy, however, if you rest your fingers lightly on the side of your pet's abdomen and exercise great patience, you should be able to feel the unborn kits moving inside the mother, and then you will know for certain that your ferret is pregnant.

BIRTH AND CARE OF THE KITS

Most ferret mothers have no trouble giving birth and can usually manage the situation with little or no help from you. If your pet trusts you and is not an unusually nervous animal, she may not mind if you watch, but even the friendliest, most gentle ferret mother does not like to have her babies handled, so it is best to avoid handling them unless it is necessary.

A few ferrets, especially those having their first litter, don't seem to know what is happening to them; they may even get confused and run into the litter pan to give birth to the first kit. In these cases a little guidance from you may save the kits from her inexperience. It is an old wives' tale that a mother will kill her kits if you touch them, and you may handle them soon after they are born without harming them. Some mothers will be like Melinda—if you pick up a kit she'll politely take it away from you and put it back into the box where it belongs. Other ferrets will bite you if you even put your hand *near* their babies, so you should proceed with caution until you know how your pet is going to react. A friend of mine was unceremoniously nipped on the nose for merely *looking* at McGuinn's newborn kits!

When the kit is expelled from the birth canal of the mother it is enclosed in a fluid-filled membranous sac called the amniotic sac. If the amniotic sac has not been broken and pushed aside during the birth, the mother must lick it away from the face and nose so that the kit will be able to breathe. Some inexperienced mothers will fail to do this, and the kit consequently will suffocate. If your female has not removed the sac within a minute or two after the kit has been born, you can help her by using the corner of a clean, damp washcloth to gently wipe the membrane from the kit's face. Within a few minutes the kit should begin to cry, and hopefully its mother will take over and care for it!

Some ferrets just don't seem to make good mothers and will eat each kit in the entire litter just as soon as it is born. This cannibalism does not seem to be affected in the least by the presence or the absence of the owner during the births. The only way to save the kits from such a mother is to take them away from her as they are born and give them to another female who is expecting kits of her own within the next day or who has just recently given

1. Melinda with her babies Scooter and McKendree shown at play in a municipal park swing. Although only nine weeks old in this photograph, the babies are already half of their full adult size. 2. The actively intelligent and inquisitive look of an adult ferret is captured well in this view of an adult female.

birth to a litter. If such a female is available she will readily adopt the kits and raise them along with her own.

I have known several ferret mothers who showed no interest whatsoever in their first litter of kits. Instead, they tried to mother their owner or other adult ferrets in the same household. The neglected kits died, but fortunately when second litters were born to these females they responded appropriately and turned out to be very good mothers.

The kits may be born anywhere from five to ten minutes apart to several hours apart. If the mother is upset it may cause an increase in the time between births. Occasionally the last kit or kits will be born as much as a day or more later than the others! A litter can contain as few as one kit and as many as 13 or 14 kits, with the average litter being about six or eight. One mother was reported to have had a litter of 22 kits, but this is extremely rare!

The babies appear pink and hairless when they are born but are actually covered with a very thin sparse layer of fine white fuzz which becomes apparent once they are fully dry. They are born with their eyes and ears sealed shut.

After the kits are born it may be several hours before they begin to nurse. If they aren't nursing by that time it may be that the mother is not producing any milk. In this case there is nothing you can do, and the kits will die unless they can be given to a foster mother to raise.

For the first several weeks after her babies are born the mother will remain with them all of the time, leaving the box only to eat and to use the litter pan. During this time the kits grow amazingly fast! As they get bigger the white fuzz grows thicker until they begin to appear white instead of pink. At this point in their development you won't be able to tell the difference between Siamese, white-foots, and sables, but you can tell whether there are any albino kits by looking at the sealed eyelids. If the kit has dark eyes you will be able to see a dark spot through the thin eyelid; the absence of such a spot means that the kit has red eyes and is an albino. If the kit is not an albino, the white fur will gradually darken as the kit grows older; it will turn a pearly gray and then a gray-brown.

When the kits are about three weeks old, especially if the litter is large, you should begin putting a soft mush in the nest box for them several times a day. The mush should be made up of canned cat food mixed with Esbilac or some other mother's milk replacement product which can be purchased in most pet stores. Even though the kits won't have opened their eyes at this age, they will already have very sharp little teeth and will eat the semi-solid food in addition to nursing from their mother. This will help take some of the burden off the mother. Giving her this relief is desirable because, despite her increased appetite and the large quantities of food she consumes, she will gradually lose weight and will usually be quite thin and run-down by the time the kits are completely weaned at six or seven weeks of age. If you neglect to put food in the nest box for the babies, the mother will frequently do this herself by carrying food to them from her own dish.

The young kits are very messy eaters, and, although their mother will clean them, you will have to clean their nest box and bedding frequently. If you are using a cardboard carton you may have to replace it several times a week. Be sure to take out the old food when you put in fresh food so that the kits won't get sick from eating food which has soured or spoiled.

WEANING

The kits should be weaned at about six weeks of age. You may want to wean them a few at a time by taking away the largest ones first and then one or two each day until they have all been separated from their mother. This will give her a chance to dry up and stop producing milk gradually, which will be more comfortable for her.

You can continue to feed the kits canned cat food mixed with Esbilac, but this should be supplemented with dry cat chow within about a week after weaning.

FALSE PREGNANCY

If your female goes through a false pregnancy, she will most likely begin to behave like a mother at the end of what would have been the six-week gestation period. Since she has no babies

1. Individual temperaments vary among ferrets and other household pets as well, but in the main ferrets and other pets get along well—especially if they have no reason to be jealous of one another. Here Beagle and ferret both share owner Bonnie Bergmeier's lap. 2. The body of the ferret should be supported properly when the animal is being lifted or carried.

82

of her own to care for she will probably adopt, and this can be a trying period for everyone involved. If there are no other ferrets in the house she may choose *you* to be the baby and follow you around, lick you incessantly, and otherwise just generally make a pest of herself. If there are adult ferrets around she will most likely drive them crazy by licking them, washing their ears, and trying to drag them off by the scruff of the neck.

When Melinda had a false pregnancy she adopted McGuinn's babies and helped McGuinn take care of them. Everything went well for the first several weeks; both mothers stayed in the nest box with the kits almost all of the time. As the kits got bigger and more demanding though, McGuinn started wanting to take a rest from nursing them and tried to nap outside the box occasionally. Melinda, however, included McGuinn among her adopted litter and refused to let McGuinn leave the box. Every time McGuinn got out Melinda grabbed her by the scruff of the neck and hauled her right back in! Melinda was so persistent at this that she finally had to be locked *out* of the cage. In addition, the method of closing the cage had to be changed from leather ties to metal snaps, because she soon learned to untie the leather knots with her teeth while hanging from her paws on the side of the cage. Then she would push the door open with her nose and go back in! This maneuver usually took her a *very* long time, but she always persisted because she wanted so much to get back to her "babies"!

2

McGuinn is shown here in side (1) and front (2) views with actor David Carradine. In these photos McGuinn is shown with a full mask; because of hormonal changes brought about by her being spayed, she has never grown another full mask.

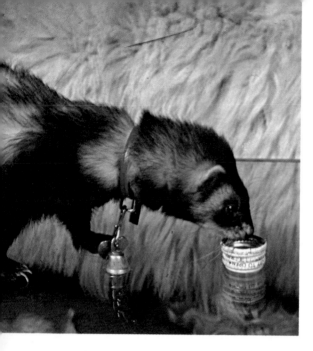

Ferrets are perky and playful whether amusing themselves with inanimate objects like a bottlecap (left) or with other ferrets (below).

Ferret
Play
And
Personality

Ferrets, like their otter cousins, are especially fun-loving and good-natured. They are natural little clowns, and most remain as playful as kittens throughout their lives. They enjoy playing with other ferrets as well as with people, dogs, cats, and other pets. Ferrets don't always need playmates, however; they will also play alone with their toys or perhaps, one might suspect from watching them, with an imaginary friend.

Ferrets are easily amused and, when feeling especially frisky, will do a "dance of joy," skittering sideways with mouth open in mock attack. At such times their fur stands straight out from their bodies, making them look like a big ball of fluff as they bounce from one end of the room to the other, often carelessly

bumping into walls and furniture in the process. Numerous worried ferret owners have telephoned me in a panic because they mistook this rather crazy behavior of their newly acquired kit for convulsions, rabies, or some other unspecified but terrible sickness. They were always relieved and somewhat surprised when I explained that their pet was only playing!

Ferrets are usually silent, but sometimes while dancing about they will emit a soft hiss or make a little chortling or clucking noise which sounds very much like they are talking "gibberish." Young kits are the most vocal and make progressively less sound as they get older.

Each ferret has its own distinct personality with unique preferences and characteristic habits. The relationships they form among themselves and with other animals as well their own favorite games and toys are as varied and different as their personalities.

Melinda prefers to play with Sally but would rather sleep with McGuinn, to whom she is the most attached. If McGuinn is not around she will usually nap by herself or on my lap rather than with either Sally or McKendree. McGuinn, on the other hand, will sleep with any of the other ferrets but won't sleep on my lap unless Melinda is already there. Sally will occasionally nap with my Siamese cat BoJeangles but usually prefers to snooze **alone** or with one of the other ferrets.

BoJeangles tolerates all of the ferrets but generally considers them to be pests because they delight in chasing her and nipping at her ears and tail. When she does condescend to play with them it is usually from the top of a chair where they can't reach her and she can reach down and bat at them with her paws. The ferrets love this game and jump up at her, trying to nip her foot as she swipes down at them.

My neighbor's cat, Chloe, has an entirely different attitude about the three ferrets she lives with. One of them, Ratso, is her best friend. They spend hours wrestling and roughhousing together like two kittens, and after Chloe gives Ratso a thorough washing she cleans her own fur and they curl up together to sleep. Chloe will occasionally play with Joco, one of the other ferrets, but she and Matilda, the oldest ferret, can barely tolerate each other and always keep a large distance between themselves.

Joco and Matilda are good friends but Ratso doesn't care that much for either of them and spends most of her time with Chloe. (My neighbor suspects that Ratso may think she's a cat!)

One of my girlfriends has two ferrets, Corkey and Scooter. Her Beagle, Beanie, loves both of the ferrets and enjoys wrestling with them and carrying them around in her mouth. Scooter likes Beanie and will frequently seek her out to play, while Corkey will quickly disappear under the sofa when he sees the dog approaching. Corkey does, however, occasionally like to make a sneak attack on Beanie's wagging tail!

Ferrets are bold and fearless and love to play "chase" or "hit-and-run" with anyone they can get to play with them. I know of one ferret who lives on a farm in Georgia who got into the habit of chasing the family horse when he discovered that he could get the horse to run from him. One day when the ferret nipped at the horse's leg the horse refused to be intimidated and instead of running away stepped on the ferret, breaking the little fellow's back. In time the ferret recovered completely, but he never tried to chase the horse again.

A little three-year-old boy I know in New Jersey, Christopher, is a much better chase companion than a horse. His ferret, Wendy, runs after him until she "catches" him, gives him a gentle nip on the heel, and then runs away—which signals Christopher's turn to chase her. (Christopher's parents are always there to see that neither playmate gets too rough with the other.)

Ferrets don't restrict their chasing to animals. Michael, a ferret in California, chases motorcycles every time he gets the chance (although he's never been able to catch one), and all of my ferrets think it's great fun to chase the vacuum cleaner!

Ferrets also love to tease. Melinda and McGuinn enjoy teasing my two skunks, Eli and Elliott, which they do by chasing them around the apartment and leaping over and onto their backs while trying to hold on. In this way they sometimes get a "skunk-back" ride from Eli, who squeals as he runs along, making it all the more fun for the ferrets. When the skunks aren't in the mood to be teased they respond by hissing and stomping their feet, which only serves to excite the ferrets more. When the skunks have had enough, however, they bite—not hard enough to do any

1. Melinda rolls over to ask for a toy and then (2) puts it to good use after having received it. 3. McGuinn and Melinda roughhousing with BoJeangles, a Siamese cat that knows them well. It would not be safe to let ferrets mix it up this way with unfamiliar animals.

2

3

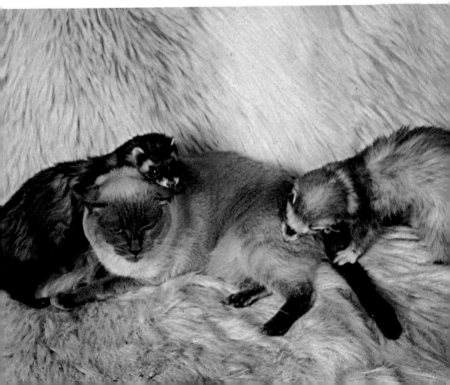

damage but hard enough to convince the ferrets that they mean serious business. At this point the ferrets quickly back down and go away in search of another form of amusement.

Unlike cats most ferrets get along well together from the first time they meet. I have never seen ferrets fight when introduced to one another—they usually appear to be overjoyed to see each other and begin to play almost immediately.

When I go downstairs to my neighbor's apartment I bring along my ferrets to play with her three ferrets and Chloe the cat. My pets enjoy visiting, but their first stop is always the food bowl. Perhaps they hope to find something more interesting than what they had for breakfast at home! In addition to knowing where dinner is the animals use the same pan and, since the ferrets don't cover up their feces like a cat does, Chloe spends a lot of time house-cleaning after her guests.

Ferrets don't always need playmates and will play with a wide variety of toys including the home-made or makeshift kind. Most ferrets are extremely fond of rubber squeak toys such as the kind made for dogs and cats. They like to chew these toys and will frequently chew until they have eaten a hole in the rubber. When this happens the toy should be thrown out and replaced with a new one, or else your pet may begin to swallow bits of rubber which can eventually block his intestines and kill him. I recommend the latex rubber toys because, although they are a little more expensive than the ordinary rubber toys, they don't chew apart as quickly and last longer.

Ping pong balls make good toys. Because ferrets are fast animals capable of "turning on a dime," they can easily keep up with the ball as they roll it along the floor with their noses. This has the effect of making them look like hockey players and is especially interesting when several ferrets are playing with the same ping pong ball.

McGuinn's favorite toy is a soda bottle cap, which she likes to push around the house with her nose. When it gets stuck in the corner she picks it up with her teeth and carries it back to the center of the room, where she puts it down and continues with the game. None of my other ferrets think of a bottle cap as a toy, but like all ferrets they enjoy crawling through tubes or tunnels of any sort, including your shirt or pants leg.

Ferrets, for all their high powered energy when awake, are amazingly sound sleepers. They bounce around in high gear until they "run out of gas" and literally "drop in their tracks" and fall asleep. Because they fall asleep so suddenly they sometimes end up sleeping in strange and unusual places. It is not uncommon to find a baby ferret sleeping draped across the side of his food bowl or litter pan, dangling half in and half out, or plopped down in the middle of the floor. Frequently it is possible to pick up a ferret, especially a baby ferret, who has fallen asleep in this manner and shake it, turn it over into various positions, and yell at it without getting any response whatsoever. The animal appears totally limp and lifeless and sometimes the breathing is almost undetectable. The first time you find your ferret kit in such a condition of sound sleep may be very frightening, because aside from having a warm body the ferret certainly appears to be dead. The first time I had such an experience I shook the baby for over a minute to no avail. However, when I put some food underneath his little nose he miraculously and instantaneously "came alive," much to my relief.

Ferrets are intelligent and fast learners and can easily be taught to do tricks. I taught my pets to roll over by offering them food as a reward. They soon learned on their own to use this action as a sort of language and began to roll over without any prompting from me whenever I had something they wanted to eat, look at, or play with. Melinda went even further and turns around and rolls over to tell me when she wants the door opened, up or down, to see what I'm doing, to get something I have, and even to get a kiss. She uses this language to say so many different things that frequently when she walks up to me and turns around and rolls over I have absolutely no idea whatsoever what she wants!

Ferrets do so many interesting things that it would be impossible for me to mention them all—and even if I could I wouldn't because it would take some of the fun out of discovering for yourself what your pet in particular likes to do and play with. (Try putting down a big bowl of water and watch your ferret to see what happens!) At any rate, I hope you enjoy your little critter as much as I have enjoyed mine, and I hope that this book will have been helpful to you.